National Association of Negro Musicians, Inc.

HONOR NIGHT

THURSDAY, AUGUST 2

MAUDE ROBERTS GEORGE, Presiding

Program

Piano: Concerto No. 3 in C Minor
    Oland Gaston, The Florence B. Price Guild, Chicago
    Marl Young, Second Piano; Walter Gossette, Organ

Introduction of Madam Anita Patti Brown

Solo: Care Selve   .   .   .   .   .   Handel
    My Heart Ever Faithful   .   .   .   Bach
            Clara Bolton

Introduction of William L. Dawson, Composer
    Chorus: Out in the Fields   .   .   .   Dawson
        William L. Dawson, Conductor

Introduction of Marion Adams
        Martha Anderson
        J. Harold Brown, Composer

Solo: (recording) Return Victor   .   .   .   Verdi
            Nadine Brewer
    Recorded by Harold White McCoo, Hartford, Conn.

Introduction of W. C. Handy
    Cornet Solo

Introduction of Florence B. Price
    Three Piano Ensemble
        Concerto in One Movement   .   .   F. B. Price
        Nannie S. Reed
            Grace W. Tompkins
                Wilhelmena Alexander

Introduction of Scholarship Winners
    Peggy Pierson   Nadine Brewer   Annie Dolly Thomas

WHO IS
Florence
Price?

Schirmer Trade Books
A division of Wise Music, the trading name of Music Sales Corporation

Exclusive Distributors:
Wise Music USA
180 Madison Avenue, 24th floor, New York, NY 10016, USA

Wise Music Group Limited
14-15 Berners Street, London, W1T 3LJ, UK

Music Sales Pty. Limited
Level 4, Lisgar House, 30-32 Carrington Street,
Sydney, NSW 2000, Australia

ISBN-13: 978-1-7365334-0-6

Library of Congress control number: 2021940294

Copyright © 2021 Kaufman Music Center

Consulting Editor: Gill Evans
Graphic Designer: Lora Findlay

Printed by Replika Press PVT Ltd, India

WHO IS
Florence
Price?

**WRITTEN AND ILLUSTRATED BY STUDENTS OF THE SPECIAL
MUSIC SCHOOL AT KAUFMAN MUSIC CENTER, NYC**

ACKNOWLEDGEMENTS

This project would not have been possible without

Kate Sheeran, Executive Director of Kaufman Music Center
for her unwavering support and belief in this project from the beginning.

Katie Banucci Smith, Principal of Special Music School
for her encouragement and trust.

Deb Schreir for her guidance and eye for color.

Marcos Balter, Rachel Sokolow, and Steve Smith
for their early enthusiasm about our project.

Robert Thompson and Julia Snowden for sharing our dream of bringing
this book to the world and helping us to make it a reality.

James Hirschfeld, Nathalie Joachim, Seth Parker Woods, Marisa Bolson,
and Natalie Oshukany for their thoughtful engagement.

All of the teachers, staff, supporters, and families that work
to make Special Music School the kind of place
where a project like this can take flight.

FOREWORD

When my dear friend Kate Sheeran, Executive Director of the Kaufman Music Center, told me about this project, I knew I wanted to be involved, and I am honored to have been asked to contribute to this book. Not only do I feel deeply connected to Florence Price's legacy through my own life's work and identity, but I also believe in young people's capacity as teachers, historians and creative visionaries, their voices as essential to our collective perception. If we can see more clearly through their eyes, we can see into a brighter and more inclusive world.

   This book represents a snapshot into the beautiful minds of children when they are given a chance to fully investigate their history and interests. They share within this recounting of Price's life, a pure enthusiasm for music and the desire to know the true experience of this iconic composer. Perhaps the most inspiring aspect of this book is how the writers were able to recognize the complex social context of Price's life, diving in to the core issues of racial and gender discrimination she faced while pursuing her passion for music. The writers' passion certainly comes through and it is clear that they learned a valuable lesson and have passed this treasure on to us that is at once investigative, honest, and generous. I want to congratulate and thank the young creators, their mentors, teachers, and supporters for bringing this beautiful publication into the world. They have reminded us with their telling of the life of Florence Price that when we pay attention to the full story of our history, we can continue to be more empowered and inspired.

Jessie Montgomery, Composer
Chicago Symphony Orchestra Mead Composer-in-Residence 2021–24

In 2009, a couple bought an old house outside of Chicago. In the attic, they found boxes filled with yellowed sheets of music. Every piece was written by the same woman – Florence Price.

"Who is Florence Price?" they wondered.

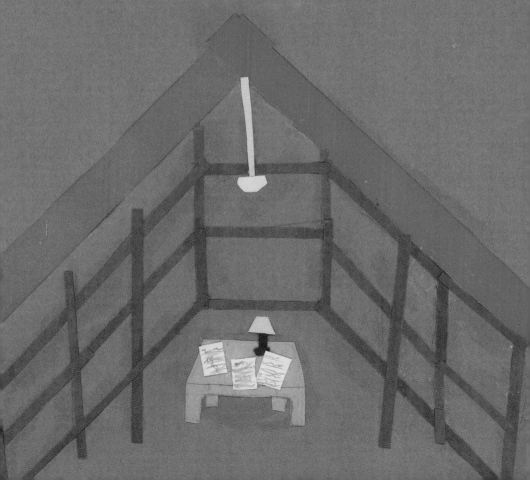

In 1887, a girl named Florence was born in Little Rock, Arkansas. Her father was a dentist and her mother was a piano teacher.

Her parents did not know that their baby girl would grow up to become a brilliant composer.

Florence's house was filled with music as she grew up. She loved to play the piano like her mom. Her fingers could make music come to life.

Sitting at the grand piano, little Florence had big dreams.

When she was four, Florence played her first concert. Her fingers flew across the keys as people watched, amazed.

She was bursting with talent, ready to share her dreams with the world.

Florence's mind was filled with music, but she had a big question.

She was a girl and her skin was a different color than so many of the composers she knew about. Could she grow up to be a famous composer, too?

When Florence was only eleven, her first piece was published. Was it possible that Florence's music could change things?

Now she was even more determined. Florence worked her hardest in everything she did. She wrote and wrote and studied and studied.

When Florence was fourteen, she graduated with the highest grades in her class.

"Wow! Who is Florence Price?" people asked.

But Florence wanted to be known for more than just her grades. She wanted people to know her music.

Certificate of Completion
Florence Price

Soon, Florence moved to Boston to study music at the New England Conservatory. In no time, the director of the Conservatory noticed how hard she worked. He was amazed by how much she cared about music.

"Where does it come from?" he asked Florence. "I hear it inside of me every day," she replied.

After two years, Florence was asked to publish another composition.

"Soon the world will hear my music!" Florence thought, hope growing in her heart. She happily accepted the offer and ran straight to her desk to keep writing.

Dear Mr. Price,

As she grew older, Florence's heart was not only filled with music but with love for her daughters. She became a piano teacher to support her family.

Now she had to write at night and began to compose her first symphony. Florence would make music any spare minute she had. She was so busy that it seemed impossible to find the time to finish her symphony.

When she accidentally broke her foot she joked, "I found it possible to get extra days to write my piece. But oh, dear me, when will I ever be able to break a foot again?"

Florence wanted an orchestra to play
her symphony when it was finished. She
entered competitions and wrote letters
to many conductors.

   She began to think she might never hear
her music performed. Because of racist
views not one orchestra was willing to play
her symphony.

   Nevertheless, she continued writing letters
and hoping.

Late into the night, Florence sat at her
piano and wrote music from the bottom
of her heart.

One morning, Florence got a letter from
Frederick Stock who was the conductor of
the Chicago Symphony Orchestra. He wanted
to perform her symphony.

Florence was overjoyed. "Maybe there is
hope after all," she said to the rising sun as

In 1933, Florence's first symphony was performed in Chicago. The audience watched, entranced. There were so many people!

The violins sang, the trumpets rang and people cheered when the final note sprang in the hall. Florence beamed.

Soon other orchestras played her work and her music became so popular it was played on television.

The American Society of Composers, Authors and Publishers invited her to become a member.

At last her music was known and heard by the world. Florence's dream had come true.

Many years later, Florence's neighbors noticed something was missing. Florence's piano had fallen silent. After that her beautiful music was rarely heard. Many of her works were even thought to be lost.

But then, in 2009 a couple bought an old house outside of Chicago. In the attic, they found boxes filled with yellowed sheets of music. Every page was written by the same composer, Florence Price.

"Who is Florence Price?" they wondered and with that, a new story began.

Today, Florence's music can be heard all around the world, just like she dreamed of when she was young.

If someone asks, "Who is Florence Price?" you can tell them.

Florence B. Price

BIOGRAPHY

Florence Beatrice Price (née Smith) was born in Little Rock, Arkansas on April 9th, 1887 to Dr. James H. Smith, a successful dentist, and Florence Irene Smith (née Gulliver), an educator. The Smiths belonged to a group of well-educated, middle-class Black Americans who thrived in Little Rock in the late 19th Century. The youngest of three siblings, she described their mother's heritage as "French, Indian [Native American], and Spanish" and her father's as "Negro, Indian [Native American], and English." Though their ancestry was mixed, because of the "one-drop rule" that dominated American society at the time, the whole family was considered "colored."

As prominent members of the community who enjoyed relative affluence, the Smith family hosted many important artists, musicians, and thinkers. Young Florence was able to begin studying music in earnest at an early age and excelled in her studies, graduating as valedictorian of her high school class at age sixteen. From 1903-1906, she attended New England Conservatory of music, one of the handful of prestigious music conservatories at the time that would accept non-white students. To further shield her from the racism she was likely to face as a Black woman in Boston, her hometown was listed as "Puebla, Mexico" upon enrollment. At NEC, she performed many piano and organ concerts and recitals at the famed Jordan Hall. After graduating with two degrees in 1906, she returned to the South and quickly established herself as an educator and private teacher. Already estranged from his wife, Dr. Smith died in 1910. Soon after, Florence's mother relocated to Indianapolis where, accepted as a white woman, she seems to have cut ties with her family in Arkansas.

A portrait of Florence Price as a young woman taken by Kettering and Reynolds Studio in Little Rock, Arkansas [Special Collections, University of Arkansas Libraries]

A portrait of Florence Price [Special Collections, University of Arkansas Libraries]

In 1912, Florence married a young lawyer named Thomas J. Price. They had three children, the first of whom died shortly after his birth. Though she did compose throughout this time, she was primarily working to support her family through teaching. By the late 1920s, her husband's law career was faltering and racial tensions in the Jim Crow South were boiling over. The Price family, like many others at the time, fled this racism and violence in what is now called the Great Migration and settled in Chicago. Though Chicago would be the backdrop for the most fruitful compositional period of Florence's life, it did not afford Thomas the same success. Financial strain and abuse led to their separation and divorce in 1931.

In 1932, Price entered four pieces in the Rodman Wanamaker Music Contest. Her *Symphony in E Minor* and *Sonata in E Minor* both won top prizes in their categories and two other pieces received honorable mentions. A lucrative and prestigious prize, her wins helped to solidify her place as one

Portrait of Florence Price with Sixteen Other People at 1934 Party in Honor of Maude R. George taken by Worthington Studios. [Special Collections, University of Arkansas Libraries]

of America's most important Black composers of the time. The following year, the Chicago Symphony Orchestra performed her *Symphony in E Minor* at the 1933 World's Fair and would go on to perform her Piano Concerto in One Movement the following year. Though institutions steeped in a culture of white supremacy would largely refuse to program her music in her lifetime, she was never truly forgotten, particularly among the Black musicians who kept her name and her legacy alive. Now, the uncovering of her manuscripts has excited a new generation of musicians and scholars, and young audiences in concert halls around the world are hearing her work for the first time.

FURTHER IDEAS

There are some big ideas in this book that are important to talk about including representation, race and fulfilling our dreams. Here are some questions to begin further discussion with a younger audience:

How do you think Florence's life might have been different if she was a different race or gender?

Can you think of a time you achieved something that you weren't sure you could, like Florence? What made it hard? What were the steps to achieve it? Who were the helpers along the way?

How could you use art to help you to express your inner thoughts and emotions, like Florence?

What do you think it would it be like if Florence Price composed today? How do you think her story might be different? How might her story be the same?

SPECIAL MUSIC SCHOOL

Founded in 1996, Special Music School is a public-private partnership between Kaufman Music Center and the New York City Department of Education.

Our K-12 school combines comprehensive, forward-thinking music instruction—including private lessons, classes, and ensembles—with a rigorous academic curriculum.

Each year, 335 students from across New York City receive this education without the financial barriers usually associated with the study of music.

The young authors of this book exemplify the possibilities that come when we open doors to comprehensive music education.

This project was born when our middle school students set out to research Florence Price's life and came up frustratingly empty-handed. While there are a few articles about Florence written for adults, we couldn't find any resources about this remarkable composer's life written for a younger audience. And so, we set out to create our own.

Like Florence, our middle schoolers know that representation matters – and they wanted to create a resource that would have inspired young Florence herself.

As we researched, wrote, and illustrated, some students also learned to perform Florence's pieces, bringing her art to life in our classroom.

We hope you have enjoyed learning about Florence's remarkable journey as much as we have.

For more information go to:
www.kaufmanmusiccenter.org/sms

This book was collaboratively written and illustrated by the middle school students at Special Music School and their teacher Shannon Potts.

Rebecca Beato and Nikita Gontarczyk were the lead illustrators.

Sixth Grade:

Jack Belmonte
Cobie Buckmire
Santiago Del Curto
Eliot Flowers
Griffin Frost
Sasha Grossman
Gretchen Kamm
Beatrice Lageschulte
Silvia Nicholson
Sebastián Núñez
Margo Pantoga
Hazel Peebles
Sophia Shao
Alma Wosner

Seventh Grade:

Caden Castro-Kudler
Anna Kesselman
Jonah Kwon
Rosalia Malik
Aubrey Mills
Gabriel Moore
Melissa Mosley

Yumi Park
Mack Scocca-Ho
Sacha Williams
Philina Zhang

Eighth Grade:

Liam Attebury
Rebecca Beato
Jonathan Berroa
Zachary Berz
Evie Brimberg
Dashiell Cain
Isabella España
Nikita Gontarczyk
Kaya Harada
Kaden Jones
Indigo Ogiste
Sadie Pine
Michael Richardson
Jesse Schopflocher
Mildred Tomppert
Tiffany Tsui
Zachary Udin
Vaishnavi Venkatesh

SELECT WORKS

Ethiopia's Shadow in America (1932)
Sonata in E Minor (1932)
Symphony No. 1 in E Minor
Fantasie No. 1 in G Minor (1933)
The Mississippi River (Suite) (1934)
Piano Concerto in One Movement (1934)
String Quartet No. 2 in A Minor (1935)
Violin Concerto No. 1 (1939)
Symphony No. 3 in C Minor (1940)
The Oak (1943)
Symphony No. 4 in D Minor (1945)
I am Bound for the Kingdom (1948)
(For and Dedicated to Marian Anderson)
Adoration (for organ) (1951)
Five Folksongs in Counterpoint (1951)
Violin Concerto No. 2 (1952)

All pieces available at:
www.wisemusicclassical.com

VIOLIN CONCERTO No. 2
Florence B. Price
ASCAP

VIOLIN II.

MAY, 1952.